apple

D1083725

MONSTERS & MYTHS
HALF MAN, HALF MONSTER

By Gerrie McCall and Lisa Regan

Gareth Stevens
Publishing

Please visit our Web site, www.garethstevens.com. For a free color catalog of all our high-quality books, call toll free 1-800-542-2595 or fax 1-877-542-2596.

Library of Congress Cataloging-in-Publication Data

McCall, Gerrie.
 Half man, half monster / Gerrie McCall and Lisa Regan.
    p. cm. — (Monsters & myths)
 Includes index.
 ISBN 978-1-4339-5003-2 (library binding)
 ISBN 978-1-4339-5004-9 (pbk.)
 ISBN 978-1-4339-5005-6 (6-pack)
 1. Monsters. 2. Metamorphosis—Folklore. I. Regan, Lisa. II. Title.
 GR825.M15 2011
 398.24'54—dc22

                                        2010033445

Published in 2011 by
Gareth Stevens Publishing
111 East 14th Street, Suite 349
New York, NY 10003

Printed in the United States of America

CPSIA compliance information: Batch #CW11GS: For further information contact Gareth Stevens, New York, New York at 1-800-542-2595.

Table of Contents

Adlet

FUR
With a red dog as their father, the adlet all have a reddish tinge to their fur.

TEETH
The adlet's teeth are dog-like, with extended canines and sharp incisors for biting and tearing flesh.

CHEST
An adlet's chest is big and muscled, and the heart of a wild animal beats inside. This creature can run constantly without getting tired.

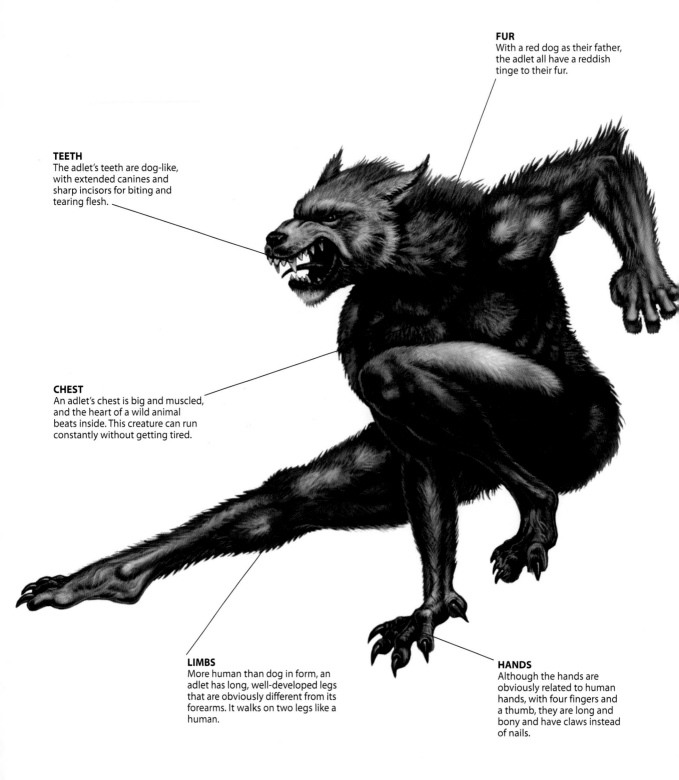

LIMBS
More human than dog in form, an adlet has long, well-developed legs that are obviously different from its forearms. It walks on two legs like a human.

HANDS
Although the hands are obviously related to human hands, with four fingers and a thumb, they are long and bony and have claws instead of nails.

The adlet is part human and part canine, with a fearsome beast of a dog as a father. Initially there were just five of them, but they bred and produced more of their race. An adlet is bloodthirsty, and preys on both humans and animals. They can even be cannibals, eating other dogs. When they first hunt down their prey, they go for the victim's throat and drink the fresh blood. Mostly, they continue to eat the flesh and insides of their victim. If possible, they hunt together to make it easier to trap their prey.

ACTUAL SIZE

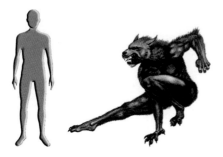

The story goes that an Inuit woman married a giant red dog and became pregnant with his children. She was obviously forced out of society for this unnatural act. Ten children were born covered with fur, and closely resembled puppies as much as human babies. The terrified woman sent five of them on a boat to Europe, where they formed the basis of the "white races," as the Inuit called them. The remaining five grew to be the ferocious creatures known as adlet.

WHERE IN THE WORLD?

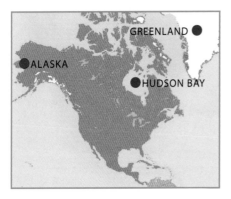

The Inuit people who tell tales of the adlet live in the remote north, in the United States, Canada, and nearby islands.

DID YOU KNOW?

• **The adlet are part of Inuit folklore, and their story is known in and around the Arctic Circle, including Alaska, the east Canadian coast, and Greenland.**

• **In Greenland and Baffin Island (off the east coast of Canada), the creatures are known by the name "erqigdlit." They are said to be the offspring of the original adlet.**

• **The tales sometimes treat the erqigdlit as literally half human, half dog, with the body and face of a person and rear legs of a canine. If they see a human they will give chase and make sure they catch and kill to get their fill of meat.**

• **Some stories suggest that the adlet's mother married a werewolf, rather than an actual dog.**

Antmen

EYES
An ant's two eyes are made up of many sets of eyes in each "eyeball," giving the antmen superb vision to spot an enemy.

JAWS
These vicious jaws are a combination of an ant's scissor-like bite, which opens and closes sideways, and a mouth full of vicious biting teeth.

EXOSKELETON
The outer skeleton of an ant acts as superb protection for its whole body. It has jointed parts to allow it to move, just like a suit of armor.

LEGS
The antmen's six legs are heavily muscled with enormous clawed hands. They can hold weapons in four of them as they rear up on their two hind legs.

In Greek legend, the antmen were a race of warriors, half ant, half human, who fought in the Trojan War on the side of Achilles. The god Zeus created them to repopulate the island of Aegina after plague had wiped out nearly all the people. The island's king, Aeacus, was the son of Zeus and pleaded with his father to give him new forces to fight against the Trojans. It is said that he pointed to an army of ants swarming around a tree and asked for them to be turned into men. This hybrid troop of ferocious warriors served him with a loyalty and devotion often seen in the insect world.

The antmen were led into battle by a mighty warrior called Patroclus. They raided the city of Troy—a fortified city thought to be invincible—without a thought for their own lives. To gain entry, they linked their toughened limbs together to form a ladder, and climbed over each other to reach the top of the city walls. Swarming through the streets, they met the Trojans head on, showing no fear. The Trojans slashed through the antmen in great numbers but even more attacked them. The antmen were a formidable army that just didn't give up fighting.

ACTUAL SIZE

WHERE IN THE WORLD?

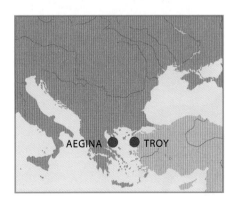

AEGINA ● ● TROY

The antmen lived on Aegina in the Aegean Sea, off the coast of mainland Greece, and stormed Troy, which is in modern-day Turkey.

DID YOU KNOW?

• An ordinary ant's legs are strong and fast. If transformed into a human, he could run as fast as a racing horse. Ants can lift 20 times their own body weight, too—so an antman is a force to be reckoned with.

• Ants are already armed by Mother Nature. Some of them can squirt acid, while others have a vicious sting.

• The battle of Troy is told in Homer's *Iliad*, a famous poem about the final weeks of fighting between the warrior Achilles and King Agamemnon.

• Killer ants make great monsters for horror stories. They have appeared in several movies (such as 1977's *Empire of the Ants*) and in Marvel Comics where Ant Man is a scientist who invents a headpiece to make ants follow his orders.

The Beast of Gévaudan

TAIL
The beast's tail is extremely long and heavy, capable of knocking over or wounding a human adult.

HEAD
The long muzzle contains many huge, pointed teeth. Its ears are small and lie flat on its head.

FUR
Although different accounts describe the beast in different colors, it is generally thought that it is reddish brown, with a gray or white chest.

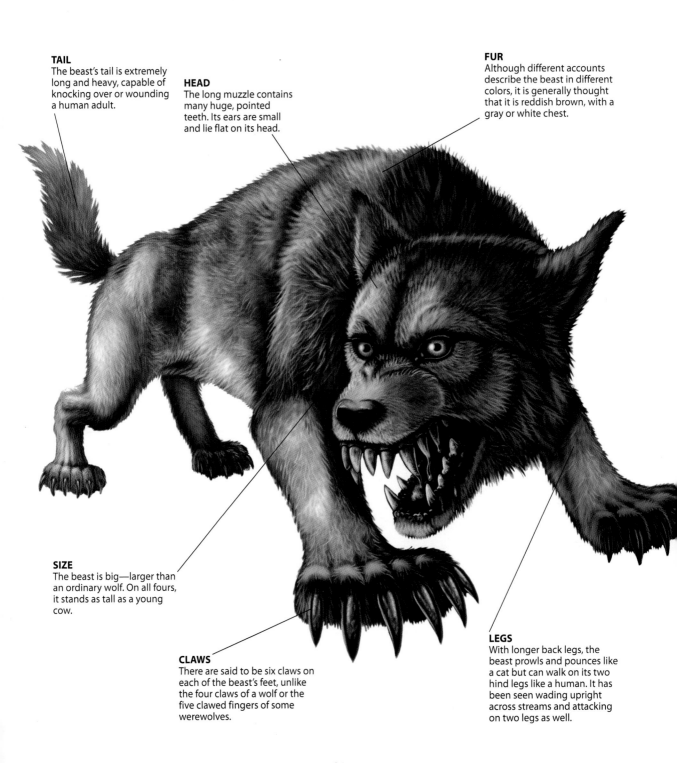

SIZE
The beast is big—larger than an ordinary wolf. On all fours, it stands as tall as a young cow.

CLAWS
There are said to be six claws on each of the beast's feet, unlike the four claws of a wolf or the five clawed fingers of some werewolves.

LEGS
With longer back legs, the beast prowls and pounces like a cat but can walk on its two hind legs like a human. It has been seen wading upright across streams and attacking on two legs as well.

The beast of Gévaudan, or la bête du Gévaudan as it is known in France, was a wolflike creature that preferred the taste of humans to the meat of sheep and cattle. It would walk past a field of cows to attack people (usually children and women) in villages and forests. Some think the creature was really a hyena, a lion, a bear, or a panther. Many thought it was a werewolf. They told tales of a sorcerer who could take the form of a giant wolf that crushed its victims' heads, drank their blood, and ate their flesh.

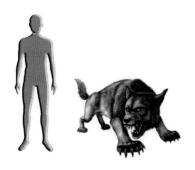

ACTUAL SIZE

As the beast roamed the countryside killing and eating its victims, the villagers decided to hunt it down. They armed themselves with pitchforks and knives but only managed to scare away the beast. The deaths continued, so King Louis XV sent his troops to track down the monster. Two of them dressed up as women to act as bait. They saw the beast several times, and fired at it, but it always got away. Eventually, a group of men shot the beast with a silver bullet, and the attacks on villages finally stopped.

WHERE IN THE WORLD?

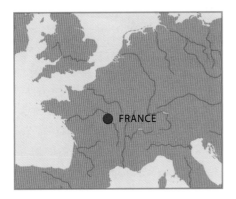

FRANCE

All of the beast's killings took place in the 1760s in Gévaudan in France. The area is now part of the département de la Lozère.

DID YOU KNOW?

• **The beast's first attack at Gévaudan was near a forest, where it charged at a woman but was fought off by her herd of cattle and bulls with their horns. A month later it returned and killed a teenage girl.**

• **Some of the beast's victims were found with their clothes carefully removed and laid over their ravaged bodies.**

• **After its death, the beast's stomach was cut open. Many human bones were found inside.**

• **At times, the beast approached people who were on their way to church, leading to stories that the creature was the devil attempting to stop people from worshipping God.**

HALF MAN, HALF MONSTER

Bogeyman

NOSE
This is wide and fat, ideal for sniffing out young victims.

EYES
Large, dark, and bulbous, the bogeyman's eyes are adapted to coping with the low light levels found under the bed and inside bedroom closets.

FINGERNAILS
Long and terrifyingly sharp, these weapons rip through bedclothes to reach petrified victims cowering underneath.

SKIN
The bogeyman's skin is covered in warts and boils and he likes to pass them on. If you have a wart, the bogeyman might have paid you a visit.

Once you switch off the bedroom light at night, your room suddenly turns into an unfamiliar place of strange shapes and eerie sounds. This is the domain of the bogeyman. One of the most common and widely feared monsters of North America, he's most likely to appear when you're in bed asleep. Angry parents sometimes threaten their children with a visit from this ogre.

ACTUAL SIZE

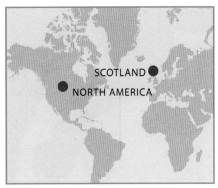

A young boy lies in bed, too frightened to move as moonlight streaks through the curtains and throws eerie shadows across his blankets. His big brother had warned him that the bogeyman would get him if he was naughty. He had seen his brother dressing up as a monster for a Halloween party, and so he expects to get a scary visit. Then, out of the corner of his eye, he notices a shadowy form taking shape in the light streaming from a widening gap in the doorway. The door opens fully and there appears a gigantic form silhouetted against the light. Convinced that his brother is playing a trick, the boy throws back the covers and leaps on to the bed to confront him. "Stop it! It's not funny," the boy screams. But, relentlessly, the figure shuffles closer. As the mysterious form looms over his bed, the boy begins to wonder if it really is his brother after all…

WHERE IN THE WORLD?

SCOTLAND
NORTH AMERICA

The bogeyman is found mainly in North America, where many towns and districts have their own legends about this horrible being. Bogeyman tales are also told in Scotland, where stories of "bogeys" abound.

DID YOU KNOW?

• **The word "bogeyman" may have come from Scotland, where mischievous goblins are called bogles, bogeys, and boggarts.**

• **There is a bogeywoman who haunts the midwestern United States, where she scratches on bedroom windows to scare small children. England also has a bogeywoman tale. Jenny Greenteeth haunts the county of Lancashire, where she preys on children who play too close to streams and ponds. Green slime on the water's surface is taken as a sign of her presence.**

Jé-Rouges

EYES
The most noticeable feature of this werewolf is its eyes, which glow red in the dark.

EYEBROWS
In their human form, they have thick eyebrows that meet in the middle. The eyebrows remain noticeable and bushy even when in werewolf form.

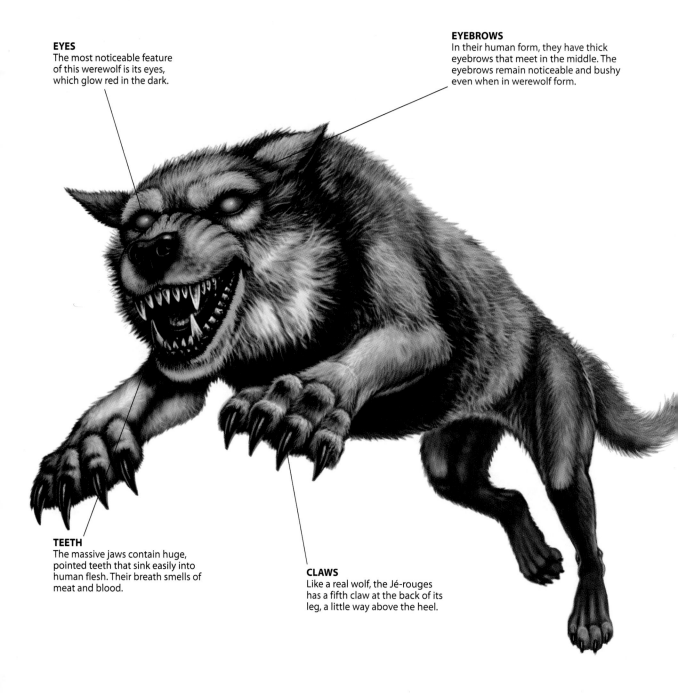

TEETH
The massive jaws contain huge, pointed teeth that sink easily into human flesh. Their breath smells of meat and blood.

CLAWS
Like a real wolf, the Jé-rouges has a fifth claw at the back of its leg, a little way above the heel.

The Jé-rouges is a werewolf spirit from the Caribbean nation of Haiti. They are created when a human gives himself over to evil forces or voodoo leaders in return for being able to change form. It is said that they can change into anything, either plant or animal. The Jé-rouges werewolf chooses the body of an unsuspecting person and possesses them each night. They transform into a cannibalistic wolf-like creature that must feed on flesh.

ACTUAL SIZE

Unlike many werewolf myths and legends, the Haitians believe that the Jé-rouges is quite vampire-like and enjoys biting people to transform them into more of its own kind. These creatures are not stupid—in fact, they are notoriously cunning. One of their favorite tricks is to wake a mother from her sleep. The werewolf asks her, in her groggy state, whether they have her permission to take her child. Of course, the mother is not really awake enough to know what is happening, and is as likely to say yes as she is to refuse and hurry to protect her children as they sleep. If she says yes, Jé-rouges may take the life or just the soul of her child.

WHERE IN THE WORLD?

HAITI

CENTRAL AMERICA

Tales of Jé-rouges are told throughout the French-speaking country of Haiti, which is on the island of Hispaniola in the Caribbean.

DID YOU KNOW?

• **This creature's name comes from a distortion of the French for red eyes: "les yeux rouges." "Les yeux" is pronounced "lay jer."**

• **It is said that the monster will turn back into its human form if you throw an iron, steel hoop, or chain over its head while it is transformed into a wolf.**

• **Many Haitian people believe in werewolves and warn their children against them. They tell tales of transformed creatures who look around the neighborhood at dusk, trying to find unlucky children to pounce on.**

• **At birthday parties in Haiti, the children try to take the piece of cake farthest from them. This superstition is supposed to stop them from being turned into a Jé-rouges.**

Lobisomem

HEIGHT
Although transformed from humans, many lobisomem are extremely tall when they rear up on their hind legs.

BODY
A lobisomem's body is completely covered in fur. Quite often it is pale gray in color, making it glow spookily in the light of the moon.

FACE
When fully transformed, a lobisomem's face is totally wolf-like, with an extended muzzle containing long, pointed teeth. Its eyes may glow red or yellow when it hunts.

LEGS
Unlike some types of werewolf, these creatures hunt on four legs, prowling across country and pouncing on all fours. They have paws instead of feet and hands.

Lobisomem are the werewolves of Portuguese and Brazilian folklore: their name comes from the Portuguese word "lobo," which means "wolf." They are often said to be tortured by their own condition, feeling distraught at what happens when they change. By the light of a full moon, they become vicious, strong carnivores, either capturing live victims who are out alone or digging up bodies from new graves to eat them.

The easiest way to become a werewolf is to fall prey to another werewolf's attack. A single bite will cause the victim to become infected. Many lobisomem attacks are frenzied and vicious enough to kill a person, which is a merciful release from a lifetime of misery every full moon. It is said that any person with eyebrows that meet in the middle, claw-like fingernails, or an unusually long third finger is a werewolf. Many South American tales say that the seventh son in a family will be cursed to change into a werewolf.

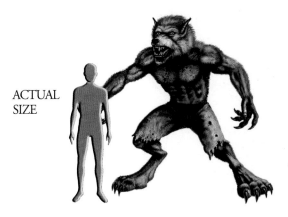

ACTUAL SIZE

WHERE IN THE WORLD?

PORTUGAL

BRAZIL

Lobisomem are native to Portuguese-speaking people, in the European country itself and in its former colony, Brazil.

DID YOU KNOW?

• Like many supernatural creatures that assume a real-world form, cursed werewolves have no tail.

• Modern tales say that lobisomem can be killed by a silver bullet, but the original folktales were around long before guns with metal bullets were invented.

• If a werewolf is killed with a silver object through the heart, it will return to its human form.

• If you can catch a werewolf, you may be able to cure it. Hurting its paws will change it back into its human form. It will have wounds on its hands and feet which must be kept open with hot candle wax. If they are dressed like this for three Sundays, the werewolf will be driven out.

HALF MAN, HALF MONSTER

Loogaroo

SKIN
As part of her transformation into a vampire, a loogaroo must take off her skin to reveal her bones and muscles inside.

FACE
Even without a covering of skin, her face shows her age. Her features are shrunken and withered.

GLOW
In readiness for her night travels, the loogaroo has a faint glow of light around her skinless body.

HABITS
Like many other types of vampire, the loogaroo is obsessive. She can be stopped from entering a house by sprinkling sand in front of the doorway. She should take so long counting the grains that daylight comes before she can attack.

In Haiti and other islands of the West Indies, a loogaroo is an old woman who has made a deal with the devil in return for magical powers. The problem is, to keep her side of the deal, she has to supply the devil with fresh blood every night. It can come from animals or humans, but if she fails to feed her diabolical business partner, he will take some of her blood instead—which will eventually kill her. It is said that these women can shape-shift into the form of a goat.

As night falls, hunting time begins for the loogaroo. First, she proceeds to her local "devil tree"—a type of silk-cotton tree, or Jumbie tree, found in the West Indies. There, she removes her skin, folds it up very carefully, and hides it by turning it into a ball of sulfurous fire. Then, she travels through the darkness as a flickering blob of light. She can enter her victim's house through any crack, then sucks up the blood she needs to keep her pact with the devil.

ACTUAL
SIZE

WHERE IN THE WORLD?

LOUISIANA

CARIBBEAN

The loogaroo is talked about in many Caribbean countries, including Haiti and Grenada, and in the southern U.S. state of Louisiana.

DID YOU KNOW?

• If the loogaroo is injured while in her animal form, the wound will show when she regains her human body.

• Check out the shadow of any suspected loogaroo— she may well cast a shadow in the shape of an animal.

• The loogaroo's victims feel exhausted and— literally—drained the next day.

• Many people believe that they have seen the loogaroo's light flashing through the darkness. Some say that the loogaroo's skin can be retrieved and mashed in a mortar with salt and pepper to kill off the vampire.

• These creatures are hated by dogs, which will bark madly at them. If a person is constantly attacked by dogs, he or she may be a shape-shifter.

Manticore

STEALTH
The manticore often prowls menacingly through the forest and sneaks up on a victim with all the stealth of a big cat stalking its prey. Then, it attacks head-on.

TAIL
The monster has the long, segmented, arching tail of a gigantic scorpion—but the tip bristles with a cluster of venomous spines, not just one sting. At close quarters, the manticore wields its spiky club like a medieval knight's mace.

BODY
The beast has the body of a lion—and the strength to match.

SPINES
When the manticore shoots spines from the club on the tip of its tail, new ones immediately grow in their place.

CLAWS
Dried blood cakes the dagger-like claws, which can slash a person open with a single swipe.

FACE
Filthy, tangled hair flows from the hideous human face like a cross between an unkempt beard and the mane of a mangy old lion.

TEETH
Three rows of long yellow teeth fill each jaw and interlock when the monster sinks them deep into a victim's body.

The manticore is a terrifying beast with the body and legs of a lion, the tail of an enormous scorpion, and the hideously distorted face of a man. A merciless and ruthlessly efficient man-eater from which no victim ever escapes, it kills with wickedly sharp, flesh-ripping claws and teeth—and by firing spear-like spikes from the end of its tail. It originated in ancient Indian mythology, before entering medieval European folklore as the embodiment of evil.

ACTUAL SIZE

WHERE IN THE WORLD?

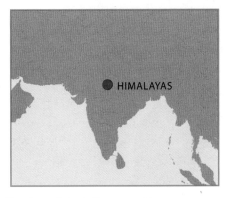

HIMALAYAS

Stories about the manticore originated from northern India in the Himalayan foothills. Tigers once abounded in these remote regions. Travelers on long, lonely footpaths between isolated villages were in constant dread of man-eaters.

A lone European merchant is on his way east to buy spices. Little does he know, but he'll never make it. The manticore springs straight for him, roaring and baring its ghastly teeth. Rooted to the spot with terror, the man barely has time to let out a strangled cry before the advancing beast is arching its tail over its head and firing a flurry of spines deep into his belly and chest. Searing pain instantly sweeps through his body. Even as the traveler falls to the ground dying, the manticore starts to devour him and greedily gulps down great mouthfuls of the innocent merchant's body. The monster eats everything: the head and clothing—even the man's meager possessions.

DID YOU KNOW?

• The word "manticore" comes from the ancient Persian word "mardkhora," meaning "man slayer."

• According to Spanish folklore, the mantiquera, or manticore, is a bearded werewolf that eats children. As recently as the 1930s, a group of peasants in a remote part of Spain attacked a traveler with a beard, believing that he was a mantiquera who had come to steal their babies by night.

Minotaur

EYES
Cold eyes glowed
with hatred.

HEAD
The great, furry head and neck
were those of a fearsome bull.

HORNS
Victims were gored to death by
the beast's huge, curved horns.

TAIL
A long, tufted ox tail
sprouted from
behind.

The Minotaur was born after King Minos angered the sea god Poseidon. Poseidon had sent a snow-white bull for Minos to sacrifice, but Minos couldn't bring himself to kill the bull. Poseidon was furious and punished Minos by making his wife, Queen Pasiphae, fall in love with the animal. Pasiphae produced a child with a grotesque bull's head and a taste for human flesh. Minos ordered the master craftsman Daedalus to make a vast underground maze to house the monster. The Minotaur was put inside, where it remained lost in the darkness. Every so often, human victims were forced into the maze as sacrifices. The Minotaur was finally vanquished by Theseus, one of the great Greek heroes.

Theseus went in search of the Minotaur, armed with a sword and a ball of thread. Tying the end of the thread firmly to a doorpost, Theseus picked his way through the tunnels of the maze, unraveling the ball as he went. He knew that, after killing the beast, he would be able to retrace his steps and escape the maze by following the thread. Suddenly, the terrible beast was upon him, snorting and charging with horns lowered. A desperate fight ensued, until Theseus plunged his sword through the Minotaur's neck, severing its head from its body.

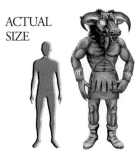

ACTUAL SIZE

WHERE IN THE WORLD?

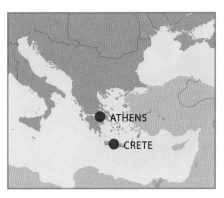

ATHENS

CRETE

The mythical Minotaur was said to have lived at Knossos, on the island of Crete in the eastern Mediterranean. Theseus, who slew the beast, came from the city of Athens on the Greek mainland.

DID YOU KNOW?

• **The story of Theseus slaying the Minotaur could be a symbolic version of real historical events, representing the Greek overthrow of Minoan power in 1450 BC.**

• **Artifacts from ancient Crete show athletes performing the death-defying bull-leaping ceremony. Each athlete would face a wild, charging bull, grasp its spiked horns, and vault or somersault over the animal's back.**

• **The Nemean lion was another Greek monster: a giant beast invulnerable to wounds.**

Mothman

FACE AND EYES
The eyes were so big and red, no other features were visible. Mothman never attacked anyone, but some people said its stare made their own eyes sore for days afterwards.

WINGS
These had a span of about 9 feet 10 inches (3 m), but no one could say if they were feathered or bat-like.

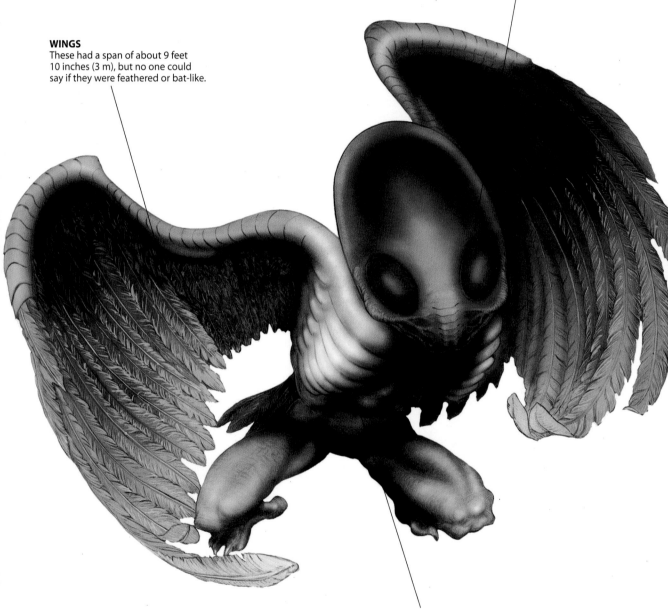

BODY
Most eyewitnesses agreed that Mothman's body was gray. Some thought it was wrinkled as well.

For 13 months in the mid-1960s, a bizarre "birdman" with glowing red eyes haunted a small town in West Virginia. This winged being had a laser-like, hypnotic stare, instilled utter dread in all those who saw it, and was said to bring disaster. Witnesses to the monster described it as being taller than a man, having gray skin, no arms, and big wings, which it kept folded behind its back when on the ground. To take off, it unfolded its wings and shot up into the air without flapping. One freezing night in December 1967, the Silver Bridge over the Ohio River in Point Pleasant collapsed at the height of the evening rush hour, killing dozens of people. To this day, monster hunters blame Mothman.

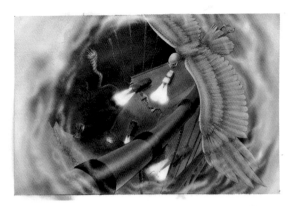

Its structure weakened by years of heavy traffic since its construction in 1928, the suspension bridge suddenly gave way, plunging cars and trucks into the icy black depths below. As the cries of people floundering desperately in the river faded, Mothman circled unseen overhead, calmly observing the terrible scene—then silently flew off into the night, never to be seen again.

ACTUAL SIZE

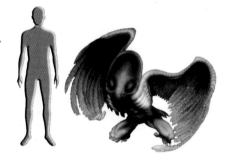

WHERE IN THE WORLD?

WEST VIRGINIA

More than 100 people claimed to see Mothman between November 1966 and December 1967 in and around the industrial town of Point Pleasant, West Virginia. Most sightings were by young couples in their cars.

DID YOU KNOW?

• **Mothman was first seen in Point Pleasant in 1961 by two people as they drove past a park called the Chief Cornstalk Hunting Ground—named after a Shawnee Indian who died fighting the British there in 1774. As he died, it's said, Cornstalk cursed the site for 200 years, a curse some people link to Mothman.**

• **A woman who saw Mothman was so frightened that she dropped her baby (who was unharmed).**

• **Many other countries have traditions of a bird-like creature that creates disaster.**

Owlman

SIZE
All the witnesses agreed that the Owlman was a huge creature, possibly 5 feet (1.5 m) tall, with gigantic wings.

EYES
Owlman's eyes glow in the dark, and are large and round (although some witnesses described them as slanted).

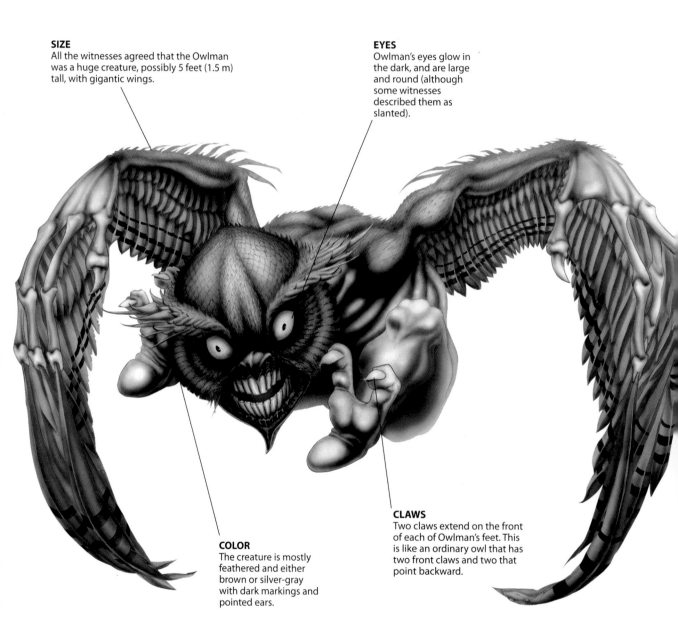

COLOR
The creature is mostly feathered and either brown or silver-gray with dark markings and pointed ears.

CLAWS
Two claws extend on the front of each of Owlman's feet. This is like an ordinary owl that has two front claws and two that point backward.

Strange things were happening in the English county of Cornwall in 1976. During the long, unnaturally hot summer, people reported UFOs, a re-emergence of the Morgawr sea monster, vicious attacks from cats, dogs, and birds—and several sightings of the Owlman. This feathered monster was first seen by two young girls, who were so frightened that their family cut short their vacation. It was seen again by several people, always around the Mawnan Church near Falmouth.

The reports continued until 1978. Then, the Owlman disappeared until 1989, when a man and his girlfriend were attacked by the creature. Stories of the Owlman had not been told for years, and the only people to think of him were locals who remembered the freakish heatwave occurrences of 1976. A young man was walking with his girlfriend one moonlit night, near the church of Mawnan Smith. He held her hand tightly and strolled as slowly as he could. As they approached the old building, they heard an unworldly shrieking noise. Both ducked in terror as an enormous, winged creature flew directly at them, with claws outstretched. They escaped unharmed—but was the Owlman back?

ACTUAL
SIZE

WHERE IN THE WORLD?

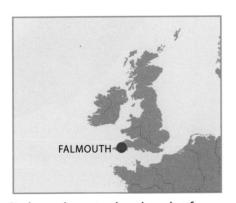

FALMOUTH

Owlman haunts the church of Mawnan Smith on the south coast of Cornwall, England, about three miles from Falmouth.

DID YOU KNOW?

• **The father of the two girls who first saw the Owlman did not go to the local police or newpapers. Instead, he told the well-known "specialist," Tony "Doc" Shields, who was also involved in the Morgawr case.**

• **The witnesses were all asked to draw what they had seen. Their pictures were compared, and each showed a similar character, although with enough differences to suggest they had not swapped stories.**

• **After the creature flies away, there is said to be a crackling or static noise heard in the trees for some time.**

• **It could well be that the Owlman is simply an extra large species of owl, such as the eagle owl. These birds grow to more than 2 feet (.6 m) with a 6-foot (.8-m) wingspan.**

Quasimodo

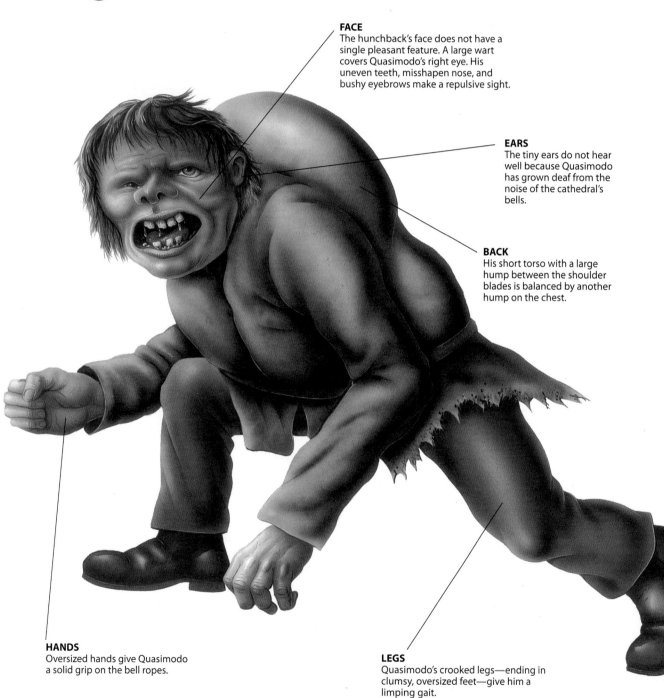

FACE
The hunchback's face does not have a single pleasant feature. A large wart covers Quasimodo's right eye. His uneven teeth, misshapen nose, and bushy eyebrows make a repulsive sight.

EARS
The tiny ears do not hear well because Quasimodo has grown deaf from the noise of the cathedral's bells.

BACK
His short torso with a large hump between the shoulder blades is balanced by another hump on the chest.

HANDS
Oversized hands give Quasimodo a solid grip on the bell ropes.

LEGS
Quasimodo's crooked legs—ending in clumsy, oversized feet—give him a limping gait.

Abandoned on the steps of Notre Dame Cathedral in Victor Hugo's book *The Hunchback of Notre Dame*, the deformed baby named Quasimodo grows up in the care of archdeacon Frollo. He becomes the bell ringer of Notre Dame. The citizens of Paris regard him as a monster. Quasimodo kidnaps Esmeralda, a gorgeous gypsy girl. She is rescued by Captain Phoebus and falls in love with him. Quasimodo is put on trial and flogged. Esmeralda pities him and brings him water. Then Frollo falls in love with Esmeralda, too. Jealous of Phoebus, Frollo stabs him and flees.

ACTUAL SIZE

Phoebus survives the stabbing, but Esmeralda is accused of attempting to murder him. She is tried and convicted of the crime. She is on the gallows, seconds away from being hanged, when Quasimodo snatches her from the platform and carries her inside the cathedral. The city leaders vote to remove the gypsy girl from Notre Dame. A group of thieves attack the cathedral to save Esmeralda. Quasimodo thinks they are there to harm her and flings stones, timber, and molten lead down on top of them.

WHERE IN THE WORLD?

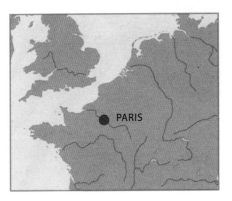

PARIS

In Paris, France, during the late 1400s, the bell ringer of Notre Dame Cathedral was none other than the hunchback, Quasimodo.

DID YOU KNOW?

• Esmeralda escapes the cathedral but is captured and hanged. Quasimodo blames Frollo for her death and throws the archdeacon off the balcony of Notre Dame.

• Quasimodo is voted the Pope of Fools in the 1482 Festival of Fools for being the ugliest person in Paris.

• The hunchback is named after Quasimodo Sunday, the first Sunday after Easter, which is the day he was abandoned at the cathedral.

• Esmeralda and Quasimodo were switched at birth. A band of gypsies stole Esmeralda from her mother and replaced her with the hideous infant Quasimodo. Quasimodo was abandoned at Notre Dame Cathedral, and Esmeralda's grieving mother became a recluse. Esmeralda and her mother are reunited just before Esmeralda is executed.

Scorpion Man

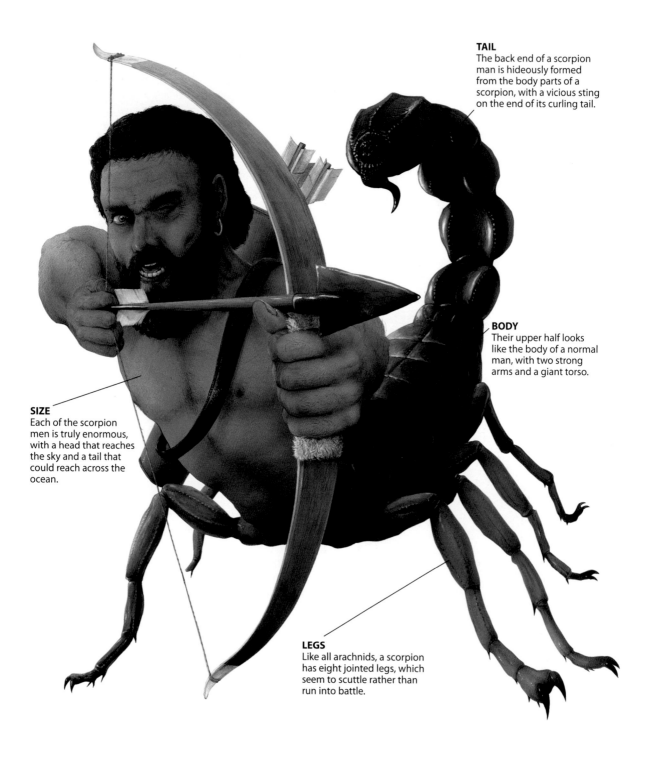

TAIL
The back end of a scorpion man is hideously formed from the body parts of a scorpion, with a vicious sting on the end of its curling tail.

BODY
Their upper half looks like the body of a normal man, with two strong arms and a giant torso.

SIZE
Each of the scorpion men is truly enormous, with a head that reaches the sky and a tail that could reach across the ocean.

LEGS
Like all arachnids, a scorpion has eight jointed legs, which seem to scuttle rather than run into battle.

These hideous creations were made by the monster Tiamat, who is a Babylonian goddess of the ocean. She mated with the god Abzu to make younger gods, but these younger gods then betrayed Abzu, and Tiamat wanted an army of beasts to get revenge. The scorpion men did exactly that, waging war against the younger gods. They are gigantic beings and awesome warriors who can fight either with their massive stinging tail, or with their deadly bow and arrow, which is said to always hit its target. It is said that their terror is awesome, and their glance is death.

The scorpion men acted as guards at the entrance to the Mashu Mountains, where the sun god Shamash lived. In the morning, they would open the eastern gate to let Shamash rise into the sky, and then welcome him back to the western gate in the nighttime, when he descended into the underworld. They warned all who tried to get through the gates that no one ever returned from inside, but allowed the Babylonian hero Gilgamesh to go in on his quest for immortality.

ACTUAL SIZE

WHERE IN THE WORLD?

MESOPOTAMIA

The scorpion men myths first circulated in Babylon in Mesopotamia, around modern-day Iraq and parts of Syria, Turkey, and Iran.

DID YOU KNOW?

• These creatures are often known by their other name, the girtablili (who are sometimes females), and also at times as aqrabuamelu.

• One of Adam Blade's *Beast Quest* books is about Sting, the scorpion man, who hides in the tunnels under Malvel's castle. There is a Monster in My Pocket scorpion man figure who holds a bow and arrow.

• Their mother, Tiamat, is also called the dragon mother, and some people describe the scorpion men as a kind of dragon race. She also gave birth to a race of mermen and mermaids.

• The movie *The Mummy Returns* features a Scorpion King at the end, who stars in the movie *The Scorpion King* played by wrestler and actor Dwayne Johnson (The Rock).

HALF MAN, HALF MONSTER

Volkodlac

SKIN
The veins can be seen near the surface of a volkodlac's skin, where patches of his tangled fur have fallen out.

EYES
A volkodlac's eyes glow in the dark and have heavy eyebrows that give him a permanently evil look. His pale blue eyes look evil even in his human form but are terrifying in his wolf's face.

JAWS
His muzzle is pointed like a wolf's, with a mouth full of large, vicious, vampire-like teeth.

CLOTHING
Look out for a wolf-skin loincloth, or an extra layer of wolf skin worn on the creature's head.

BODY
A volkodlac has the body of a wolfman: he usually walks upright but can prowl on all fours. He has the well-defined torso of a bodybuilder.

In Slavic folktales, the volkodlac spends the daytime in human form and changes into wolf form during the hours of darkness. If the werewolf is killed, it becomes a vampire. Once this happens, it can become a werewolf occasionally to satisfy its appetite for flesh and blood. If the vampire is killed and proper precautions are not taken, the cycle starts again and the creature is reborn as a werewolf. It is possible to become a volkodlac by being bitten by one, but this is rare as the monsters usually eat their victims. They feed on animals as well as people.

During the harsh European winters, the volkodlacs gather together in groups, mostly in forests. They remove their wolf skins and hang them from the trees. They might decide to release one of their kind from his curse by taking his skin and burning it. The others gather around the fire and dance and howl. This allows the chosen volkodlac to die peacefully and remain at rest.

ACTUAL SIZE

WHERE IN THE WORLD?

EASTERN EUROPE

Most tales of the volkodlacs' wickedness are told by the Slavic people of eastern Europe.

DID YOU KNOW?

• **This monster's name appears with many different spellings, such as vlklodak and vulkodlak, depending on which country you are in. The name translates as "wolf's hair."**

• **If you manage to kill this almost-indestructible beast, you should place a coin in its mouth to stop it from coming back to life in vampire form.**

• **A human with enough evil in his soul can put on a wolf skin and transform into a volkodlac. When he takes it off, he becomes human again. A person can also drink rainwater taken from the footprint of a wolf.**

• **Several Slavic stories describe how the creature can be killed by piercing its heart with a pointed stick from an aspen tree.**

HALF MAN, HALF MONSTER

Wendigo

SIZE
Reports differ on how tall the creature is. Some say the height of a man, others say 15 feet (4.6 m) tall. Its most noticeable feature is how skeletally thin it is.

FUR
Personal hygiene is not important to this devil. Its fur is matted and filthy, and smells really, really bad.

TEETH
The vicious bite of a wendigo could be enough to turn you into a cannibalistic monster—but it is more likely you won't make it that far and will be eaten.

CLAWS
Its heavily clawed hands and feet are used to grab its victims and stop them from being able to escape.

The wendigo is a North American cannibalistic monster, usually shown as thin and starving, with its bones visible under the surface of its skin. It is this chronic hunger that drives the creature to hunt for flesh to eat. It signifies the greedy part of human nature, and it's said that its hunger can never be satisfied, so it consumes more and more victims in a frenzy of gluttonous feeding. Yet, the more it eats, the bigger it grows, so it is always hungry and thin, needing more food to fill its belly.

ACTUAL SIZE

A Cree Indian by the name of Jack Fiddler spent his life tracking wendigos. He said that over the years he recognized, trapped, and disposed of 14 of the monsters. His son Joseph helped him in his mission to safeguard the local people and prevent attacks from nearby wendigos on the hunt for human flesh to eat. However, in 1907, both Jack and Joseph were arrested, tried, and imprisoned for the murder of a Cree Indian woman who they claimed had been possessed by a wendigo spirit and was going to eat members of their tribe.

WHERE IN THE WORLD?

● NORTH AMERICA

Several Native American tribes of the United States and Canada tell tales of the wendigo, especially the Algonquian-speaking peoples.

DID YOU KNOW?

• The wendigo is sometimes called the "spirit of lonely places" and lives alone in forests and isolated prairies. It tracks silently, following people through the woods.

• The creature is said to be so thin that you cannot see it from the side. You only know it is there if you meet it head-on.

• Wendigos have recently moved into the mainstream, and have been featured in TV series such as *Charmed, Blood Ties,* and *Supernatural.* There is also a horror movie called *Wendigo,* and they appear in Steven King's *Pet Sematary.*

• There is a medical condition called wendigo psychosis where the patient feels hungry for human flesh and is fearful he or she might turn into a cannibal.

HALF MAN, HALF MONSTER

Werebear

PAWS
One blow from this monster's massive paws is enough to knock its victims unconscious. Its claws are long and vicious enough to kill a full-grown man.

ARMOR
As many werebear tales come from Norse mythology, these creatures are quite often armed with an ax or may wear body armor.

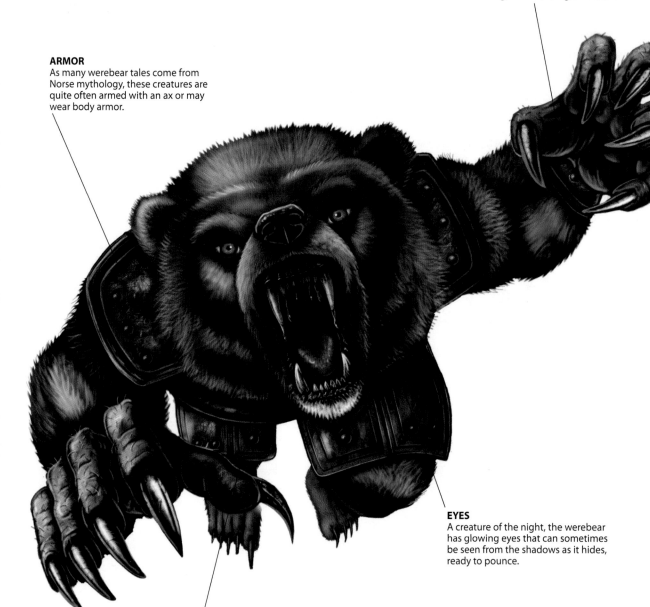

EYES
A creature of the night, the werebear has glowing eyes that can sometimes be seen from the shadows as it hides, ready to pounce.

BODY
Just as a bear is one of the most powerful mammals, a werebear is extremely strong, with huge muscles and a mighty body.

The werebear is related to the werewolf but is even more fearsome. Many countries that were home to bears also had folktales of werebears. They were strong and powerful, with signs of human intelligence, and sometimes the skills to use weapons. In Norse history, the Berserkers were a group of warriors who wore bearskins and fought so wildly that they were thought to be werebears. Like werewolves, werebears only transform at certain times, usually linked to the phases of the moon. They often show signs of extreme tiredness once they return to their human state.

ACTUAL SIZE

A werebear will often act in a bear-like way even in its human form. In one Native American story, a man called Red-breasted Turtle returned from his day's hunting with a deer to feed his family. Four times he killed a deer but was robbed of it on his way home. The man who stole the deer acted strangely, so Red-breasted Turtle lay in wait to see who he really was. He jumped out and killed the strange man. As the man died, he transformed into a bear.

WHERE IN THE WORLD?

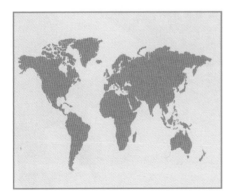

Tales of werebears are told where bears are more feared in the wild than wolves: notably North America, Russia, and parts of Europe.

DID YOU KNOW?

• Werebears are strong and fierce and extremely difficult to destroy. If one is killed, it must be burned with all its belongings, to stop it from coming back to life.

• A dead werebear's bones, once burned, should be ground into powder. This powder may be used by a holy man as a cure for the werebear's victims. It can even bring the victims back to life.

• The Berserkers got their name from the bear furs (serks) that they wore. The modern word "berserk" means furious to the point of recklessness, or showing no fear.

Weretiger

SENSES
Humans are no match for the sensitive nose, eyes, and ears of an ordinary tiger. Once witchcraft is added into the mix, a person has no chance of avoiding this animal.

LEGS
A weretiger will prowl and hunt on all fours, but can stand on two legs like a man and rear high over the head of its victims.

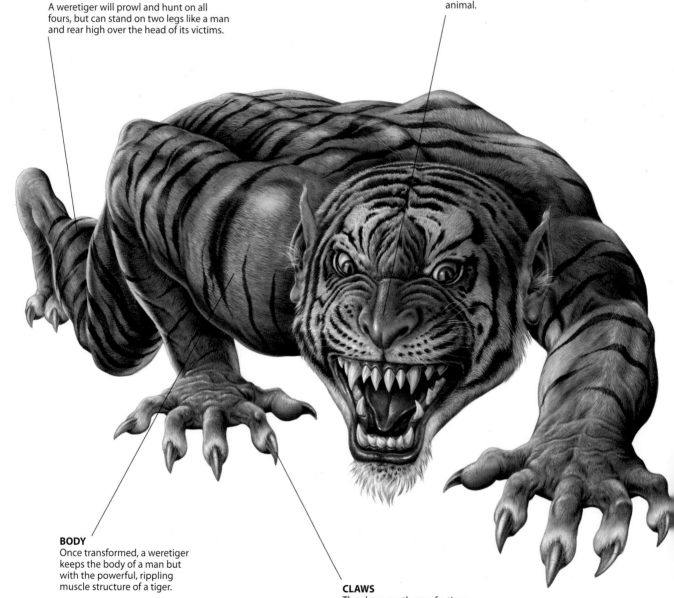

BODY
Once transformed, a weretiger keeps the body of a man but with the powerful, rippling muscle structure of a tiger.

CLAWS
The claws are those of a tiger, but they are in the strangely deformed hands and feet of a human, not the four-toed paws of a true tiger.

Like their relatives the werewolves, weretigers are shape-shifters that look human by day, but transform at night. However, a weretiger does not rely on the full moon and can change whenever it wants. A person will become a weretiger for different reasons, depending on the beliefs of the people in different areas. Some people believe that a weretiger is a powerful magician who can shape-shift as they choose. In China, people are turned into weretigers by a curse or an evil ghost. In Thailand, a weretiger is a real tiger who has fed on many people and become more human.

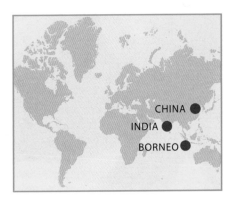

It is the belief of some Indonesians that a weretiger is a man who possesses a magical sarong, only as big as his big toe, that transforms him at night. He puts on the skirt, which becomes as large as his body, and is orange and black striped. In his weretiger shape, he hunts for victims. If a weretiger is trapped in its feline form, by the time morning comes he will have turned back to a human (but watch out for him still gnawing at his food if he is still hungry…).

WHERE IN THE WORLD?

CHINA ●
INDIA ●
BORNEO ●

Tales of weretigers occur wherever tigers used to roam in the wild: in parts of Southeast Asia, including India, China, and Borneo.

DID YOU KNOW?

• In Malaysia, the weretiger will not eat humans as long as it has enough cattle and chickens to keep it well fed. A person who is believed to be a weretiger is made to be sick. If their vomit contains feathers, it is proof of their shape-shifting.

• Any person who is a weretiger will have the reflection of a tiger, either in a mirror or in the surface of a body of water.

• Tales are told around the world of other werecats, including werelions, wereleopards, and werelynxes. It depends on the particular species native to an area.

• Certain people are said to be able to turn themselves into weretigers through spells, charms, incantations, and fasting (starving themselves).

HALF MAN HALF MONSTER
Werewolf

EYES
Keen, merciless eyes can spot victims even in the shadows.

MOUTH
A bloodcurdling howl salutes the moon and warns that the werewolf's hunt is beginning. Its fangs subdue prey and shred meat from bones easily.

EARS
The large, pointed ears hear the faintest sounds made by prey from a great distance.

BODY
Built for endurance, the muscular body stalks and chases as long as the full moon is shining.

PAWS
Strong hands and feet grip anything in this beast's path. The claws tear away any flesh not already slashed by the fangs.

Werewolves are humans with the ability to shift their shape into wolves. During the day, they are ordinary people, but a full moon triggers a terrible transformation. The person's body sprouts hair, grows fangs, and enlarges into its werewolf form. Prowling only at night, werewolves devour cattle, kidnap children, attack travelers, and destroy what they cannot eat. Once it tastes human blood, it is forever cursed. A person may not know he or she is a werewolf. Immune to aging and disease, the werewolf must eat the flesh of the living for all eternity.

Anyone can become a werewolf by rubbing his or her body with a magic potion, drinking water from the footprint of a werewolf, eating wolf's brains, sleeping under the full moon on a Friday, having two werewolf parents, or being bitten by a werewolf. Unlike the vampire, it cannot be harmed or frightened away by religious artifacts. The only way to kill a werewolf is with a silver bullet. The dead werewolf's head must be cut off and burned so that it does not return as a vampire three days later.

ACTUAL SIZE

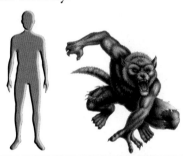

DID YOU KNOW?

• Some believe that children born on December 24 will become werewolves.

• A poisonous herb called wolfsbane can be used to ward off a werewolf.

• Injuries suffered while in wolf form will show on the skin when the werewolf returns to human form.

• The mere touch of silver to a werewolf's skin can cause burns and scarring.

• In Argentina, the belief that a seventh son would become a werewolf was so strong that many parents abandoned or killed their seventh sons. To stop this practice, a law was passed in 1920, which stated that the president of Argentina is the official godfather of every seventh son born in the country. The state awards seventh sons scholarships, and they receive gold medals at their baptisms.

WHERE IN THE WORLD?

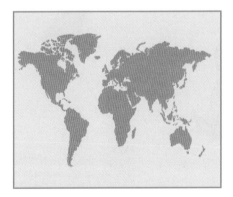

Werewolves are prevalent worldwide. In any country you visit, you may encounter a werewolf in the dark.

The Wolf Man

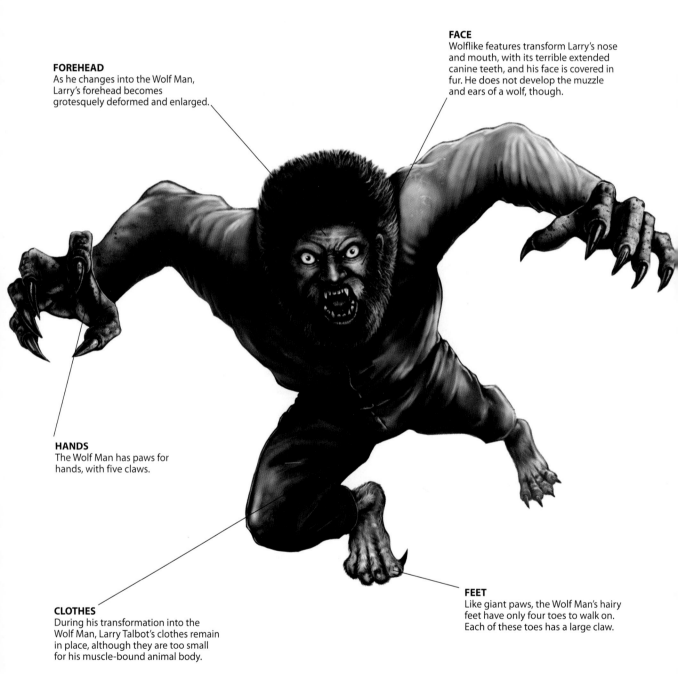

FOREHEAD
As he changes into the Wolf Man, Larry's forehead becomes grotesquely deformed and enlarged.

FACE
Wolflike features transform Larry's nose and mouth, with its terrible extended canine teeth, and his face is covered in fur. He does not develop the muzzle and ears of a wolf, though.

HANDS
The Wolf Man has paws for hands, with five claws.

CLOTHES
During his transformation into the Wolf Man, Larry Talbot's clothes remain in place, although they are too small for his muscle-bound animal body.

FEET
Like giant paws, the Wolf Man's hairy feet have only four toes to walk on. Each of these toes has a large claw.

Not just any old werewolf, the main character in a movie from 1941 is literally part wolf and still part man. Whereas other werewolves make a complete transformation under a full moon, the Wolf Man remains vaguely human in appearance. He walks on two legs, and his face is still recognizable as that of a person (although he is, admittedly, a very hairy person). While still human, he hears an old poem that will stay with him: "Even a man who is pure in heart and says his prayers by night, may become a wolf when the wolfsbane blooms and the autumn moon is bright."

A newcomer to Wales, Larry Talbot knows little of werewolves until he buys an antique walking stick decorated with a silver wolf's head. He is told that it represents a werewolf, and he hears the poem for the first time. That night, while trying to rescue a friend from a wolf attack, he is bitten—and is turned into a werewolf himself. He is doomed to prowl at night in search of prey. The Wolf Man is finally defeated by his father, who kills him with his own silver-headed walking stick.

WHERE IN THE WORLD?

WALES

LLANWELLY

The Wolf Man roams the village of Llanwelly in Wales by night, and lives in Talbot Castle during the daytime.

DID YOU KNOW?

• **Unlike many werewolves, the Wolf Man is not transformed by the light of the full moon, but only when the wolfsbane blooms in the fall.**

• **Wolfsbane is a flower said to have supernatural powers. It can turn an infected person into a werewolf if they smell, wear, or eat the plant.**

• **The Wolf Man appears in several movies after the original 1941 black-and-white movie. These later movies often change his characteristics, such as the times when he is able to transform.**

• **Not all werewolves are vulnerable to silver. Usually, this is more associated with vampires.**

• **The werewolf who bites Larry is a gypsy called Bela, a fortune-teller's son. He has suffered the curse of lycanthropy (being a werewolf) for years.**

Yowie

HAIR
Thick hair covers the beast's broad, fat-bellied frame, and this varies in color from reddish brown to near black.

HEAD
The Yowie dismembers prey with its massive, downward-curving canine teeth, and in artificial light its irises reflect red.

ARMS
The beast hurls rocks through the air and tears up small trees with its muscular arms and huge hands.

FEET
The Yowie can run three times as fast as a human, leaving long-toed, wide footprints in the dirt.

Huge, hairy, and elusive, the Yowie allegedly hides out in some of Australia's most inaccessible regions. It hunts by night, stalking kangaroos and other animals through the bush before ripping off their heads. The Yowie can move at amazing speed over rough terrain—leaping over creeks and boulders. Occasionally, it wanders close to areas of human habitation, where it watches people from dense cover, and if disturbed, the Yowie stamps its feet, beats its chest, and shakes trees until they snap. Sometimes, the creature charges at intruders: screaming and growling, displaying its teeth, and releasing an odor of rotting flesh and bad eggs. Other people have been terrorized when the beast has attacked their vehicles or hurled rocks.

▲ A couple sleep peacefully in their new home, oblivious to the world outside. The wife's pet pooch is left to roam around the garden, and it scampers over to investigate a rustling in the bushes. Suddenly, a hulking figure looms into view, sending the dog into a frenzied fit of barking. All is calm the following morning, and after breakfast, the woman goes out to feed her pet. But she calls in vain, and when the couple search carefully, her husband finds a torn and bloodied collar. It seems the Yowie devoured the yapping terrier as a snack.

WHERE IN THE WORLD?

GREAT DIVIDING RANGE ●

In the 20th and 21st centuries, Yowie sightings have been most frequent in the eastern regions of Australia, particularly in the hills and forests of the Great Dividing Range that stretches from Queensland down to Victoria.

ACTUAL SIZE

DID YOU KNOW?

• When a team of Royal Air Force surveyors landed by helicopter on a remote mountain peak in 1971, they found fresh Yowie tracks in the mud.

• In places where the creatures' prey has become scarce, people have seen Yowies scavenging on roadsides for animals killed by passing traffic.

• Yowies are immensely strong, and one startled Yowie even managed to overturn a moving Jeep.

Adlet
Area: Alaska, Greenland, Hudson Bay
Features: Face, fur, and claws of a dog; legs and upright posture of a human; muscular; reddish coloring; sharp teeth

Antmen
Area: Aegina, Troy
Features: Half ant, half human; two "eyes" made up of many eyes for better vision; has an ant's scissor-like jaw; vicious teeth; exoskeleton acts as body armor; six muscled legs

The Beast of Gévaudan
Area: France
Features: Looks like a wolf, but larger; reddish-brown fur; huge, pointed teeth; can walk on its hind legs like a human; six claws on each foot; long, heavy tail

Bogeyman
Area: North America, Scotland
Features: Large eyes that see well in the dark; wide, fat nose; long, sharp fingernails; skin covered in warts

Jé-Rouges
Area: Haiti, Central America
Features: In human form, they have bushy eyebrows; in wolf form, they have glowing red eyes, massive teeth, and claws

Lobisomem
Area: Portugal, Brazil
Features: Werewolf; extremely tall; covered in pale gray fur; full wolf face; eyes may glow red or yellow

Loogaroo
Area: Louisiana, Caribbean
Features: Old woman; takes her skin off; glows

Manticore
Area: Himalayas
Features: Body and legs of a lion, face of a man; dagger-like claws; three rows of yellow teeth fill each jaw; tail of a scorpion with many venomous stingers

Minotaur
Area: Athens, Crete
Features: Body of a man, head of a bull; eyes glow; furry neck and head; curved horns; long, tufted ox tail

Mothman
Area: West Virginia
Features: Taller than a man; wings; gray body; big, red glowing eyes

Owlman

Area: Falmouth, England

Features: Possibly 5 feet (1.5 m) tall; eyes glow in the dark; mostly covered with brown or silver feathers; two claws on the front of his feet

Quasimodo

Area: Paris

Features: Wart covers his eye; uneven teeth; misshapen nose; oversized hands; crooked legs with oversized feet; short torso with a hump on his back and front; tiny ears

Scorpion Man

Area: Mesopotamia

Features: Upper body looks like man; the back end has the body parts of a scorpion including the tail, stinger, and eight legs; head reaches the sky and tail could reach across the ocean

Volkodlac

Area: Eastern Europe

Features: Human by day, wolf by night; eyes glow in the dark; vampire-like teeth; muscles are well defined; wears extra wolf skins for clothing

Wendigo

Area: North America

Features: Skeletally thin; covered in smelly fur; huge claws on hands and feet; may be as much as 15 feet (4.6 m) tall

Werebear

Area: North America, Russia, Europe

Features: Changes to bear from human; may wear body armor; powerful, muscular body; massive paws; eyes glow at night

Weretiger

Area: China, India, Borneo

Features: The body of a man with the powerful muscles of a tiger; tiger claws on strange, human hands; can stand on two legs

Werewolf

Area: All over the world

Features: Human by day, wolf at the full moon; muscular body; fangs; strong hands and feet with claws

The Wolf Man

Area: Wales

Features: Still looks human, though his face changes; bigger teeth; paws with claws for hands and feet; muscular body rips his clothes

Yowie

Area: Australia

Features: Fat belly; covered in thick hair; huge teeth; eyes can reflect red light; big feet and hands

Glossary

allege: to claim as true

bulbous: round like a bulb

chronic: lasting a long time

devour: eat quickly and forcefully

embody: to represent

frenzy: wild activity

gluttonous: wanting to eat or drink a lot

gypsy: wanderer

hygiene: health and cleanliness

immune: able to withstand

keen: very good

medieval: having to do with the Middle Ages

molten: melted

naughty: bad

oblivious: not being aware

prevalent: happening often

reckless: wild

recluse: someone who does not visit with people

relentless: does not stop

transform: change from one thing to another

For More Information

Books

Emmer, Rick. *Bigfoot: Fact or Fiction?* New York, NY: Chelsea House, 2010.

Hugo, Victor. *The Hunchback of Notre Dame.* Retold by Michael Ford. Brighton, England: Book House, 2007.

McCaughrean, Geraldine. *Theseus.* Chicago, IL: Cricket Books, 2005.

McCormick, Lisa Wade. *Mothman: The Unsolved Mystery.* Mankato, MN: Capstone Press, 2010.

Pearce, Q. L. *Wendigo.* Detroit, MI: KidHaven Press, 2009.

Troupe, Thomas Kingsley. *The Legend of the Werewolf.* Makato, MN: Picture Window Books, 2011.

Web Sites

Death Raptor aka Owlman
animal.discovery.com/tv/lost-tapes/death-raptor/
Read and watch videos about the Owlman.

Victor Hugo
www.hugo-online.org
Find out more about the man who created Quasimodo.

Werewolf
animal.discovery.com/tv/lost-tapes/werewolf/
Discover more about the werewolf myth.

Index